Hugh MacDiarmid

by
Edwin Morgan

C. M. Grieve, or 'Hugh MacDiarmid' as he is best known, has written under both names, and in this he seems to be following a Scottish custom (one could instance 'Lewis Grassic Gibbon' and J. Leslie Mitchell, or 'James Bridie' and O. H. Mavor). But whether two, or more than two identities meet in his work, there is no doubt that he is one of the most far-ranging, original, and remarkable poets of his time.

Apart from his natural abilities, and the recognizable quality of his best work, Hugh MacDiarmid has a noted historical importance in Scotland in the double aim he proposed to himself in the 1920s, of reviving and extending the use of Scots into a full medium of expression, and of initiating a new, vigorous, and modern phase of Scottish poetry and (in company with others) of Scottish literature in general.

From the startling economy of his early lyrics, through the developed, highly imaginative symbolism of *A Drunk Man Looks at the Thistle*, to his later, more provocative experiments in very long 'poems of knowledge', Hugh MacDiarmid has never ceased to explore what is there to be explored—experience, language, ideas, books. If his work is *sui generis*, it also has considerable variety of appeal, and a depth of challenge to the interested reader.

Edwin Morgan was born in Glasgow in 1920 and is at present Titular Professor of English at Glasgow University. His own volumes of poetry include *The Second Life* (1968) and *From Glasgow to Saturn* (1973), and he has also published collections of his verse translations from various languages (*Rites of Passage*, 1976) and of his literary essays (*Essays*, 1974). He received the Cholmondeley Award for poetry in 1968, and has had a number of Scottish Arts Council Book Awards.

Acknowledgements: Our thanks are due to Christopher Murray Grieve for permission to quote from his work and to Jonathan Cape and University of California Press for their permission to quote from *Selected Essays* of *Hugh MacDiarmid* and *Lucky Poet*. We also wish to acknowledge the following publishers of Hugh MacDiarmid's work: William Blackwood & Sons Ltd—*Sangschaw*, *Penny Wheep*, *A Drunk Man Looks at the Thistle*, *To Circumjack Cencrastus*; Faber & Faber Ltd—*Annals of the Five Senses*; Routledge & Kegan Paul—*The Hugh MacDiarmid Anthology*. We further wish to thank the Editor of *The Guardian* for allowing us to quote from an article by Hugh MacDiarmid, and Duncan Glen of Akros Publications for the use of the frontispiece portrait which originally appeared in *An Afternoon with Hugh MacDiarmid* (1969).

The Buildings itself

Duncan

HUGH MacDIARMID

HUGH MacDIARMID

by

EDWIN MORGAN

Edited by Ian Scott-Kilvert

PUBLISHED FOR
THE BRITISH COUNCIL
BY LONGMAN GROUP LTD

LONGMAN GROUP LTD
Longman House, Burnt Mill, Harlow, Essex

*Associated companies, branches and
representatives throughout the world*

First published 1976
© Edwin Morgan

*Printed in Scotland by
T & A Constable Ltd, Edinburgh*

ISBN 0 582 01258 9

HUGH MacDIARMID

I

'HUGH MACDIARMID' is the pen-name of Christopher Murray Grieve, who was born on 11 August 1892 in Langholm, a small town in Dumfriesshire, a few miles from the Scottish-English border. His father was a local postman, his grandfather a power-loom tuner in a tweed mill. Although his literary and intellectual interests were to take him very far from Langholm, both geographically and spiritually, he has more than once written with an enthusiastic glow about his boyhood environment.

The delights of sledging on the Lamb Hill or Murtholm Brae; of gathering 'hines' [raspberries] in the Langfall; of going through the fields of Baggara hedged in honeysuckle and wild roses, through knee-deep meadowsweet to the 'Scrog-nit' wood and gathering the nuts or crab-apples there; of blaeberrying on Warblaw or the Castle Hill; of 'dookin' [bathing] and 'guddlin' [catching fish by hand, or just playing about] or making islands in the Esk or Ewes or Wauchope and lighting stick fires on them and cooking potatoes in tin cans—these are only a few of the joys I knew, in addition to the general ones of hill-climbing and penetrating the five glens which (each with its distinct character) converge upon or encircle the town—Eskdale, Wauchopedale, Tarrasdale, Ewesdale, and, below the town Carlisle-wards, the 'Dean Banks'.[1]

This country childhood, set in what he recalls as 'an almost tropical luxuriance of nature', evidently left strong impressions, for he has in many ways remained a rural poet at heart, and despite the fact that his 'faith has always been in the industrial workers and in the growth of the third factor between Man and Nature—the Machine',[2] he has not written often, or inwardly, about urban life.

But if MacDiarmid is a countryman, he is a countryman who has read more voraciously than most townees. The post office building where the family lived was also the home

[1] 'My Native Place', *Selected Essays*, 1969, pp. 53-54.
[2] *Lucky Poet*, 1943, p. 3.

of the Langholm Public Library, and the boy used to the full his free access to its 12,000-odd volumes. 'I could go up into that library in the dark and find any book I wanted.'[1] Thus began the habits of a lifetime: his unusually wide-ranging reading of books and journals, his relish (which was both didactic and autodidactic) for noting and quoting, his exploring of wisdom through recorded knowledge and fact as well as through the speculative activity of the mind.

The more formal part of his education was at Langholm Academy and later at the Broughton Junior Students' Centre in Edinburgh, and in both places he came under teachers who discerned his quality and encouraged him to write. (His tribute to George Ogilvie, his English teacher in Edinburgh, is included in *Early Lyrics by Hugh MacDiarmid*, ed. J. K. Annand, 1968.) By 1911 he was working as a journalist in Wales, and from then until he joined the army in 1915 he had jobs with various papers in Langholm, Clydebank, Fife, and Angus. He also showed his early interest in politics by joining the Independent Labour Party when he was sixteen, and by doing research for the Fabian Society. After war service with the Royal Army Medical Corps in Salonika, Italy, and France, he married Margaret Skinner and settled in Montrose, working with the *Montrose Review*, becoming a Labour town councillor and a Justice of the Peace, before he moved to London in 1929. During the twenties he was extremely active with his own poetry as well as with journalistic writing of all kinds, and his continued involvement with public affairs is seen in his being a founder member of the National Party of Scotland and of the Scottish branch of PEN.[2] His editing of anthologies and magazines, his habit of writing (sometimes about himself) under several assumed names, and his ceaseless provoking of ordinary readers and literati alike, to reinvigorate their awareness of what was deleterious or hopeful about Scottish traditions, go very well to bear out his description of his own function as 'that of the cat-fish that vitalizes the other torpid denizens of the aquarium.'[3]

[1] *Lucky Poet*, p. 8.
[2] Poets, Editors and Novelists' Club.
[3] *Lucky Poet*, p. xv.

4

His years in England in the early 1930s were among the unhappiest of his life, and Kenneth Buthlay has plausibly suggested that this may 'cast some light on the increasing bitterness of his Anglophobia'.[1] It seems to have been a triple crisis: employment difficulties, the break-up of his marriage, and his new commitment to Communism. He was divorced in 1932, and in 1933 he went with his new wife, Valda Trevlyn, to live in a cottage on the island of Whalsay in Shetland, in a poor state of health and with virtually no money. The eight years he spent on that bare northern island were a major testing-time from which he emerged through patience and an indomitable spirit— and the indomitable spirit of his wife—into new phases of his life.

During the second World War MacDiarmid trained and worked as a fitter on Clydeside, and later was first engineer with a ship in the Merchant Service. In 1950 he was awarded a Civil List pension, and the following year he moved into the small cottage near Biggar in Lanarkshire where he lives today. Greatly increased general recognition of his work can be dated from 1962, the year of his seventieth birthday, which saw the publication of his *Collected Poems* (so-called, though very incomplete) in America and of the *Festschrift* edited by Kulgin Duval and Sydney Goodsir Smith in Edinburgh. There has always been, and there still is, disagreement about the nature and extent of his achievement in poetry, but at least there is not now that neglect which must seem the most unsuitable of all fates for his highly idiosyncratic work.

MacDiarmid's name is associated with the revival of Scottish poetry in the twentieth century to which the term 'Scottish Renaissance' has been applied—a phrase that during the half century of its use has become harder and harder to define: (are we still living in it? has it one wave, two waves, three? is it literature plus language or literature plus language plus politics?). Although MacDiarmid did not himself directly invent and apply the term in the first instance, there is no doubt that it represents what he was consciously working towards in his early poetry. In one of the most

[1] Kenneth Buthlay, *Hugh MacDiarmid*, 1964, p. 4.

straightforward statements he has made about his aims, he says:

I wanted to escape from the provincializing of Scottish literature. I wanted to carry on the independent Scottish literary tradition from the time that Burns died, for it didn't seem to me that anything of value had been done in between. I wanted to carry forward the reintegration of the Scots language, taking it a good deal farther than Burns had taken it, and at the same time to carry forward the tradition politically.[1]

It will be seen that this programme includes linguistic, political, and cultural elements. After MacDiarmid was demobilized in 1919, he found, as others did in Scotland, a sharpened sense of nationhood as one of the results of the war. His struggle to express and then to nurture this sense took him both into political action and into the development of a new poetry. The first poetry he wrote was in English, and was not particularly distinguished. Gradually and deviously, between 1921 and 1923, he began to move towards the position of believing that Scots might be revived, and carried out his own experiments in Scottish poetry.[2] What was clear to him—and it is his great historical importance to have seen this—was that the moment had come for an exploration of Scottish vocabulary and idiom quite different from the debased, sentimental, jocose, moralizing tradition of nineteenth-century Scottish verse: in other words, Scots could be placed, and worked in, against the background of European symbolism and modernism. Here, the 'national' and 'international' strands in MacDiarmid's thinking came happily together. From a deliberate study of Sir James Wilson's *Lowland Scotch as Spoken in the Lower Strathearn District of Perthshire* (1915) and John Jamieson's *Etymological Dictionary of the Scottish Language*, added of course to his own familiarity with spoken Scots as it still survived, he was stimulated into believing that 'the Scots Vernacular is a vast storehouse of

[1] 'MacDiarmid on MacDiarmid', *Guardian*, 22 February 1962; reprinted in *The Uncanny Scot*, 1968.
[2] The transition is well documented in Duncan Glen, *Hugh MacDiarmid and the Scottish Renaissance*, 1964, pp. 71-83.

6

just the very peculiar and subtle effects which modern European literature in general is assiduously seeking'.[1] The stimulus of contact with the richness of Scots, even with words that were rare, obsolescent, or obsolete, is given strong witness in an interview of 1975 where he said:

I fell in love with the Scots language and I tried to extend it . . . It was like a revelation when I wrote my first poem in Scots . . . I must have tapped some source deep in myself.[2]

The poems in *Sangschaw* (1925) and *Penny Wheep* (1926), mostly short lyrics, are the first fruits of that enthusiasm, and the former volume is one of the landmarks of modern Scottish poetry. *Sangschaw* came with a preface by John Buchan, which put the case for this new experiment rather well:

He [MacDiarmid] would treat Scots as a living language and apply it to matters which have been foreign to it since the sixteenth century. Since there is no canon of the vernacular, he makes his own, as Burns did, and borrows words and idioms from the old masters. He confines himself to no one dialect, but selects where he pleases between Aberdeen and the Cheviots . . . It is a proof that a new spirit is to-day abroad in the North.

Some readers would argue that the best of these poems— 'The Bonnie Broukit Bairn', 'Au Clair de la Lune', 'Crowdieknowe', 'The Watergaw', 'The Eemis Stane', 'The Innumerable Christ'—have not been surpassed in MacDiarmid's later work. His poetry changed so fundamentally during the thirties and forties that comparison is difficult, but there seems no doubt that these early lyrics, miniatures though they are, retain an extraordinary freshness and strangeness which come not only from lexical surprise but also from the highly imaginative mental perspectives their scenes and events disclose. 'The Eemis Stane' is a good example:

> I' the how-dumb-deid o' the cauld hairst nicht
> The warl' like an eemis stane

[1] *Scottish Chapbook*, Vol. 1, No. 8, March 1923.
[2] *Scottish Marxist*, No. 10, Winter 1975.

Wags i' the lift;
An' my eerie memories fa'
Like a yowdendrift.

Like a yowdendrift so's I couldna read
The words cut oot i' the stane
Had the fug o' fame
An' history's hazelraw
No' yirdit thaim.

how–dumb–deid: empty dead silence   *hairst:* harvest   *warl':* world
eemis stane: rocking stone   *lift:* sky   *yowdendrift:* blizzard
fug: moss   *hazelraw:* lichen   *yirdit thaim:* buried them

Part of the effectiveness of the poem depends on technical details like the subtle interlacing of rhymes (across as well as within stanzas), the repeated 'yowdendrift' which emphasizes the driving down of the snow ('This isn't just a fanciful comparison; I want you to think about the obliterating process'), the use of alliteration in 'fug o' fame' and 'history's hazelraw' to give the two unfamiliar words a sort of habitation and gain the reader's confidence. But the reverberations of the meaning, the resistance to full analysis, are another thing; in its small space the poem has a visionary, Blakean quality. The observer sees the earth like an unsteady, teetering stone, but is it a tombstone on which the record and significance of its own past are somehow inscribed, if only we could read the inscription, or is it more like a logan-stone whose very precariousness and seeming defiance of the laws of survival are its main attraction? The desire for knowledge and the appeal of strangeness, opposite as they are, are knit together. Subjectivity ('my eerie memories') as well as the apparently more objective comments of fame and history succeeds only in adding layer upon layer of interposition between us and the real. Yet the poem does not protest or take sides. It remains an image, haunting the mind, rocking there like its own eemis stane.

Many of the poems in *Sangschaw* show similar cosmic images and preoccupations. The earth 'glitters beneath the seas o' Space, / White as a mammoth's bane' ('The Man in the Moon'); the moon perches like a crow 'on the fower cross-win's / Peerin' a' roon' ' ('Moonstruck'); the planets chat together in gorgeous clothes while the earth stands like a neglected tear-streaked child ('The Bonnie Broukit Bairn'). But as the last example shows, we are never far away from earthly interests, and some of the poems have a Brueghelesque realism that was absolutely new-minted as far as Scottish poetry was concerned, after its many years of retreat from reality. An example is 'Country Life':

> OOTSIDE . . . Ootside!
> There's dooks that try tae fly
> An' bum-clocks bizzin' by,
> A corn-skriech an' a cay
> An' guissay i' the cray.
>
> Inside! . . . Inside!
> There's golochs on the wa',
> A craidle on the ca',
> A muckle bleeze o' cones
> An' mither fochin' scones.

dooks: ducks *bum-clocks bizzin':* beetles buzzing
corn-skriech: corncrake *cay:* jackdaw *guissay:* pig *cray:* sty
golochs: earwigs *on the ca':* being rocked *muckle bleeze:* great blaze
fochin': turning

The vigorous, delighted movement of the poem, as of many others in the collection, made a better case for his use of Scots than pages of argument would have done. The title *Sangschaw*, which might be translated as 'Songfest', rightly stressed the lyrical aspect, and in fact many of the poems were set to music by the composer Francis George Scott, who had been one of MacDiarmid's teachers at Langholm Academy. But the striking point about the lyricism of the verse was that it was not lax but functional, gauged, at once economical and liberated. Through it MacDiarmid was able to produce effects of macabre humour ('Crowdie-knowe'), intense human absorption ('In the Hedge-Back'), or measured meditation ('The Innumerable Christ'). Or sometimes it is an effect that is hard to describe, as Edwin Muir noted when he remarked that 'Country Life' had humour 'and yet conveys a kind of horror'. Such mixed effects, like the frequent employment of the grotesque, are very much a part of the Scottish tradition, though given new life by MacDiarmid.

Penny Wheep was put together on the same pattern as *Sangschaw:* and the ironic title ('small beer') perhaps conceals some uneasiness about repeating an earlier success. Although its best poems are on the same level as those in *Sangschaw*, the general standard is not so high. There is no doubt about the quality of 'Somersault', 'Krang', 'Cloudburst and Soaring Moon', 'Empty Vessel', 'The Bubblyjock', or 'Gairmscoile', and these cover a considerable range of reference and feeling. 'Somersault' shows the earth swinging and rushing headlong through space and praises the meaningful wildness of the huge cycles of life. In 'Krang', a world appears like a whale's carcass, stripped to the bone by the sun, this carcass in turn being likened to a white harp for a whirlwind to make music from, a song for the poet to emulate if he can. 'Empty Vessel', a simple but by no means unsubtle poem about a girl who has lost her baby and gone out of her mind, also has an unexpected cosmic touch:

> I met ayont the cairney
> A lass wi' tousie hair
> Singin' till a bairnie
> That was nae langer there.
>
> Wunds wi' warlds to swing
> Dinna sing sae sweet,
> The licht that bends owre a' thing
> Is less ta'en up wi't.

ayont the cairney: beyond the small cairn

Based on an old song ('Jenny Nettles'), itself based on a true story, this poem opens out suddenly in the second stanza into an enormous contrast to what has gone before—winds rocking worlds, light bending across the curvature of space—and yet these vast things are nothing compared to the dishevelled figure of the small human person trying to protect a child, a child which is not even there. It is very Wordsworthian, except perhaps that its opening 'I met' is a more classic gesture, a more introductory phrase, than it would be in the less impersonal Wordsworth—though the difference is slight.

'Gairmscoile' stands apart from these poems. A longer, non-lyrical, discursive, incomplete piece on the characteristics and uses of the Scots tongue, it provides in its own lively lines an apt defence of its arguments. Apart from declarations of solidarity with Wergeland, the nineteenth-century Norwegian nationalist poet with whom MacDiarmid evidently felt he had much in common—not merely the linking of language and national identity but also the world-consciousness and the running fullness of expression—it concentrates its recommendation of Scots on grounds that would appeal to the George Steiner of *Beyond Babel*:

> . . . And there's forgotten shibboleths o' the Scots
> Ha'e keys to senses lockit to us yet
> —Coorse words that shamble thro' oor minds like stots,
> Syne turn on's muckle een wi' doonsin' emerauds lit.
>
> .   .   .
> Hee-Haw! Click-Clack! And Cock-a-doodle-doo!
> —Wull Gabriel in Esperanto cry
> Or a' the warld's undeemis jargons try?
> *It's soon', no' sense, that faddoms the herts o' men.*
> *And by my sangs the rouch auld Scots I ken*
> *E'en herts that ha'e nae Scots'll dirl richt thro'*
> *As nocht else could—for here's a language rings*
> *Wi' datchie sesames, and names for nameless things.*

>   *Coorse:* coarse   *stots:* bullocks   *Syne:* then
> *doonsin' emerauds:* bright emeralds   *undeemis:* amazingly varied
>   *dirl:* ring   *datchie:* secret

These 'forgotten shibboleths' and 'datchie sesames' were what his early lyrics discovered, and something that began as a personal experiment turned out in the end to be a widely appreciated body of work from a new poet whose name was obviously one to watch. Without accepting the extreme view of MacDiarmid's poetry expressed by Iain Crichton Smith, that he 'would give away whole swatches of MacDiarmid's later work for "The Watergaw" alone',[1] one can readily feel that the poems in these two early volumes are one of the peaks of his achievement.

[1] 'The Golden Lyric', in *Hugh MacDiarmid: A Critical Survey*, ed. D. Glen, 1972.

II

For those who believe that lyrics are not enough (and MacDiarmid is certainly one of them), *A Drunk Man Looks at the Thistle* (1926) is his most potent testing-ground for a more extended and ambitious use of the imagination. While he was working on this long poem of some 2,600 lines, with great intensity and excitement, in 1925 and 1926, he sent accounts of its progress, as trailers for publication, to the *Glasgow Herald*, and these give us a useful insight into its composition and general aims. It is described as 'a gallimaufry . . . Its matter includes satire, amphigouri,[1] lyrics, parodies of Mr T. S. Eliot and other poets, and translations from the Russian, French, and German. The whole poem is in braid Scots, except a few quatrains which are in the nature of a skit on Mr Eliot's "Sweeney" poems, and it has been expressly designed to show that braid Scots can be effectively applied to all manner of subjects and measures' (17 December 1925). Two months later he writes that it is 'a complete poem . . . deriving its unity from its preoccupation with the distinctive elements in Scottish psychology which depend for their effective expression upon the hitherto unrealized potentialities of Braid Scots' (13 February 1926). In a letter to George Ogilvie on 6 August 1926[2] he makes it clear that despite some 'infernally intractable material' and some worries about overall unity— 'really one whole although many parts are detachable'—he is confident that he has uncovered new powers in the writing of this poem. Most readers would agree with him.

The poem is not tightly knit as argument or narrative, yet it does hold together, because the method of composition perfectly suits the main conception of the work. A drunk man is lying sprawled in the moonlight, looking at a huge thistle which seems to him in his befuddled state to be constantly changing its shape and being transformed into other things. So both the whisky he has been drinking and the moonlight which makes everything strange and mysterious

---

[1] Nonsensical composition.

[2] Quoted, like the above newspaper extracts, in *Early Lyrics by Hugh MacDiarmid*, ed. J. K. Annand, 1968, pp. 13-16.

combine to produce a dreamlike atmosphere. Sometimes in fact he wonders whether he *is* dreaming the whole thing. But he insists that reason does not have all the answers.

> I doot I'm geylies mixed, like Life itsel',
> But I was never ane that thocht to pit
> An ocean in a mutchkin. As the haill's
> Mair than the pairt sae I than reason yet.

doot: suspect   *geylies:* very much   *mutchkin:* half-bottle
haill's: whole is

We are not to expect the poem to move along by logical progression or logical development of ideas, nor is it going to issue in a single truth or a single conclusion. It is going to reflect the mind of the dreamer (and of its author) in its abrupt and unexpected transitions from the sublime to the ridiculous and back again. Only the force and interest of the mind behind it will give it unity. MacDiarmid was influenced by the Russian philosopher Lev Shestov (1866-1938), who wrote: 'You will at last be convinced that truth does not depend on logic, that there are no logical truths at all, that you therefore have the right to search for what you like, how you like, without argument, and that if something results from your search, it will not be a formula, not a law, not a principle, not even an idea!'[1]

The theme of Scotland is fairly pervasive in the poem, as one would expect from the title. Although the thistle becomes or is likened to many other things, it is basically the Scottish national emblem, and the drunk man looking at it is MacDiarmid's device for commenting, in a great variety of tones, on his own country. This theme is emphasized at the beginning, in satirical references to the Burns cult, and at the end, when the drunk man sees the Great Wheel of the universe, with Scotland on its whirling rim 'squattin' like a flea', and looking closer sees all the Scots, and exclaims:

> 'Mercy o' Gode, I canna thole
> Wi' sic an orra mob to roll.'
> —'*Wheesht! It's for the guid o' your soul.*'

. . .

[1] 'Penultimate Words', in his *Anton Tchekhov and Other Essays*, translated by S. Koteliansky and J. M. Murry, 1916, p. 141.

13

> '*A Scottish poet maun assume*
> *The burden o' his people's doom,*
> *And dee to brak their livin' tomb.*
>
> *Mony ha'e tried: but a' ha'e failed.*
> *Their sacrifice has nocht availed.*
> *Upon the thistle they're impaled.*'

thole: bear   *orra:* nondescript   *maun:* must

But the theme of Scotland, although it is important and helps to hold the poem together, is not the only one. The thistle itself is used as a starting-point for many other ideas. The drunk man looking at it is reminded of a bagpipe, not because it looks like a bagpipe but because it looks like the sound of a bagpipe—the leaves are like the drone and the purple flowers at the top are like 'the pirly-wirly notes / That gang staggerin' owre them as they groan'. Or he says the leaves are like alligators that have swallowed a company of Highland soldiers 'And left naethin' but the toories [pompoms] / O' their Balmoral bonnets to tell the tale'. Or it's like a huge bellows blowing out sparks; or green tides washing up to the stars; or a gargoyle, or a skeleton, or the missing link; a flash of lightning, a candelabra, an octopus, a brain laid bare, a penis, a man's nervous system, a pickled foetus, a jet of water with balls playing on top, an epileptic, the masts and rigging of a ship; or MacDiarmid himself. These comparisons show MacDiarmid's brilliant grotesque imagination, his fondness for the startling, provoking image, but they also help to keep the thought of the poem active and ready to swing off suddenly in a new direction.

In the early part of the poem the drunk man very often homes in on the thistle as a growing thing, something that suggests the source of life, the physical basis of life.

> I'se warrant Jean 'ud no' be lang
> In finding whence this thistle sprang.

The close mingling of physical and spiritual, of love and disgust; the relation of sex and thought: these ideas lead the speaker on to thinking about religion, original sin, the virgin birth of Christ, and the possibility of Christ being born again.

14

> Wull ever a wumman be big again
> Wi's muckle's a Christ? Yech, there's nae sayin'.

He often returns to this idea of a second birth, a second coming, and in a strange way he later links himself to it when he sees himself as trying to give birth to something new.

> I'm fu' o' a stickit God.
> THAT'S what's the maitter wi' me.

> *stickit:* stuck, failed

The drunk man as a god-bearer, 'rolling in agony' as he says, is an agent of human evolution, and the theme of evolution, which becomes more and more important in the later poems, has its beginnings here. It is the sense of future evolution that also distinguishes MacDiarmid's approach to this subject: his belief that every man is 'a quart that's squeezed into a pint'. Stress is laid again on the physical foundations of life; the thistle may be a 'pickled foetus' that any man would shudder from, yet even the pickled foetus has *some* existence in comparison with nothingness, absence of being. Returning to the pint-pot image, the drunk man imagines the expansion and liberation of life:

> But let my soul increase in me,
> God dwarfed to enter my puir thocht
> Expand to his true size again,
> And protoplasm's look befit
> The nature o' its destiny,
> And seed and sequence be nae mair
> Incongruous to ane anither,
> And liquor packed impossibly
> Mak' pint-pot an eternal well.

But this is still far away. Life is still full of conflicts and paradoxes, and all its opposites seem to be aspects of something still unknown, mysterious, greater than either man or God. Ygdrasil, the world-tree of Scandinavian mythology, is introduced, in another metamorphosis of the thistle, and man is no more than 'a stick-nest' in its branches which stretch from heaven to hell. Seen in a perspective of all life, man is not the goal of creation, and there may be forms of life to whom our idea of heaven is no more than the shining track of a snail on a wall. After these remote speculations, the drunk man comes back to earth, back to himself and his friends, his drinking companions, his wife, and speaks ironically about them, yet—and it is a very nice touch—he has not lost the thread, he is still thinking about evolution, but this time he casts his eye back into prehistory and makes unflattering comparisons:

> And faith! yestreen in Cruivie's een
> Life rocked at midnicht in a tree,
> And in Gilsanquhar's glower I saw
> The taps o' waves 'neth which the warld
> Ga'ed rowin' like a jeelyfish,
> And whiles I canna look at Jean
> For fear I'd see the sunlicht turn
> Worm-like into the glaur again.

een: eyes   *Ga'ed rowin':* went rolling   *glaur:* mud

These meditations on evolution are perhaps the 'philosophical' core of the poem, but they are followed by a fascinating digression, a lengthy and intricate address to Dostoevsky. Like Wergeland in 'Gairmscoile', and like Rilke and Lenin and Charles Doughty in other poems, Dostoevsky is used by MacDiarmid as an unexpected sounding-board for his ideas, and helps to densen the texture of the poem. Various things about Dostoevsky attracted him—his being a prophetic writer, his concern with ideas of being born again, the tension between belief in the exceptional man and belief in the common people. Even his gambling and his epilepsy suggest something (the 'anti-domestic' gambler, the 'saintly' epileptic) he can react to sympathetically. And of course his deep 'Russianness' appeals to the conscious Scot in MacDiarmid. Dostoevsky would have understood the drunk man's mystic localization of spiritual forces:

> And as at sicna times am I,
> I wad ha'e Scotland to my eye
> Until I saw a timeless flame
> Tak' Auchtermuchty for a name,
> And kent that Ecclefechan stood
> As pairt o' an eternal mood.

sicna: such

16

The poem as a whole has remarkable power, and more cohesion than one might expect from the somewhat hectic method of its composition, with passages being put in and taken out right up to the last moment. There are sections that could be clearer, and some that just don't quite come off (e.g. the parody passage bringing in Thomas Gray, T. S. Eliot, and John Home); there are problems, here and there, of vocabulary and syntax. But it remains a highly original poem, meaty, visionary, comic, endlessly surprising.

The year 1930 saw the publication of another ambitious (and still longer) poem, *To Circumjack Cencrastus*. This, despite some fine anthologizable sections, is generally regarded as an unsatisfactory work. The title means 'to enfold the curly snake', and the speaker in this poem begins by addressing his meditations to a huge and mysterious serpent, much as the drunk man had stared at his thistle. But here the resemblance ends. There is no real-life setting as there was in the earlier poem, and the serpent is not kept in mind, as the thistle was, throughout the body of the poem (even though it returns at the end), so that structure virtually disappears. It is far more of a 'gallimaufry' than *A Drunk Man Looks at the Thistle*, which the author described as such. The snake, as an ancient wisdom symbol, powerful, glimpsed intermittently, moving on its un-fathomed business, hard to catch or circumjack, was in itself quite a promising choice for a central image, and it had strong personal associations for MacDiarmid when he looked back to his boyhood in Langholm, where a favourite winding path was called the Curly Snake and had always haunted his imagination. 'There is nae movement in the warld like yours', the poem begins, and it goes on to praise the serpent for being always different, for having no fixed shape, for being an exemplar of change held out to inertial and complacent man. Poets in the throes of composition will sometimes catch sight of it, as an angler will see some large fish that eludes him, stretched out like a dim cloud beneath the shining small fry he easily takes. Snake—fish—cloud—the images begin to multiply. But then nothing much more is made of this, and although Cencrastus does appear now and again in the course of the poem, sometimes in the water, sometimes spreading its hood like a cobra, sometimes reaching up into the stars ('I see your coils twisted to a point / Faur ayont Ophiuchus'[1]), it is only at the end that it comes back in any meaningful way, and by that time it is too late to save the 200-page poem. Many of the Scottish and evolutionary ideas of the *Drunk Man* are repeated in *To Circumjack Cencrastus*, but without any particularly illuminating development. The author's own dissatisfaction with the poem's lack of direction and control bursts out halfway:

> (*Hell tak this improvisin'*
> *That leads a' airts and nane:*
> *A kind o' anti-poetry*
> *That is true poetry's bane!*)

airts: ways

MacDiarmid had by no means given up the desire to write long poems, and his often-expressed interest in Ezra Pound no doubt arose out of a sense of similar ambitions and similar problems in encompassing both lyric and epic modes. But probably he had no more to say at the end of the twenties in the particular kind of long poem he had devised —the 'gallimaufry' with abrupt switches of subject and the use of different styles and forms, but with a general leaning towards metre and rhyme. To get Cencrastus he might have to cast off into less charted seas.

III

During the 1930s, despite the fact that this was one of the most difficult periods of his personal life, MacDiarmid published several collections of great interest: *First Hymn to Lenin* (1931), *Scots Unbound* (1932), *Stony Limits* (1934), and *Second Hymn to Lenin* (1935). Two developments that make their appearance are a more extensive use of political and scientific material, and more poems being written in English, even although Scots was still very much employed, and indeed intensified in some poems. Politically,

[1] The constellation, 'the Serpent-bearer'.

MacDiarmid has been a hot potato to Nationalists and Communists alike, and his espousing of the Social Credit doctrines of Major Douglas, his desire for a Celtic crescent of workers' republics from Scotland to Brittany, and his continued interest in religious and metaphysical matters (*pace* statements like 'I do not believe in God at all'[1]) ensured that he would often be out of step with the machinery of dogma and party. Without denying the reality of either his Communism or his nationalism, we have to remember that he is a poet who is also a citizen rather than a citizen who is also a poet. He will sit down at a demonstration in Trafalgar Square, but he will also write:

As a Socialist, of course, I am, it should be obvious, interested only in a very subordinate way in the politics of Socialism as a political theory; my real concern with Socialism is as an artist's organized approach to the interdependencies of life.[2]

The 'interdependencies of life' are in truth his central concern, and this is clear in many of the political poems. The theme of 'Second Hymn to Lenin' is the relation of poetry to politics, the place of poetry in social evolution and the function and value of the poet relative to a revolutionary like Lenin. It expresses strongly MacDiarmid's belief in the importance of poetry; his sense that his poems ought to be 'spoken in the factories and fields', even though they aren't and are not likely to be; his emotional impatience with the 'breid-and-butter problems' of economics; his reminding of Lenin that a poet's subjects cannot be ranged in a hierarchy but must be allowed to come as they move him:

> He daurna turn awa' frae ocht
> For a single act o' neglect
> And straucht he may fa' frae grace
> And be void o' effect.

Here MacDiarmid sticks to his last with some persistence, not even giving Lenin the arguments he might be expected at some points to adduce in reply, yet making a fairly central gesture of solidarity in saying

[1] *Lucky Poet*, p. 51.
[2] *Lucky Poet*, p. 241.

> Poetry like politics maun cut
> The cackle and pursue real ends.

—Solidarity within context; but it can recall too Yeats's 'walking naked' and Eliot's 'the poetry does not matter'. Slippery fish, poets!

'The Seamless Garment' is the political poem that has been most highly regarded, though like Iain Crichton Smith, in *The Golden Lyric*, I find that despite its being finely worked out—indeed perhaps because it is so neatly worked out—it leaves less of an impact than one would expect from it. A triple analogy brings together the three 'seamless garments' of well-made tweed in a Langholm mill, the well-made poetry of Rilke, and the well-made identification of Lenin with working-class life. The poet hopes he can find the same indivisible close-woven integrity in his own work.

> The womenfolk ken what I mean.
> Things maun fit like a glove,
> Come clean off the spoon—and syne
> There's time for life and love.

It is a good poem, rooted in the life of his native place yet working through metaphors and connexions with an easy and intelligent movement.

The use of the technical background of tweed-making in 'The Seamless Garment' is a mild example of what was to become an almost obsessional attempt to bring poetry and science into close contact. Political themes are nicely allied to a certain degree of technical vocabulary in two short poems, 'The Skeleton of the Future' and 'On the Ocean Floor'. The former poem presents Lenin's mausoleum in Red Square in Moscow: a winter scene.

> Red granite and black diorite, with the blue
> Of the labradorite crystals gleaming like precious stones
> In the light reflected from the snow; and behind them
> The eternal lightning of Lenin's bones.

This small but very striking poem attains its effects through symbolic use of colour and light: the strong but sombre red and black, the colours of revolution, have within them and around them three kinds of light, the blue crystals sparkling like jewels (a treasure, something precious, underneath), the shining of the snow (suggesting Russia itself, the Russian earth), and the half-real half-metaphorical 'lightning' of Lenin's bones (the embalmed body, lit up in the interior darkness of the tomb). The uncommon words 'diorite' and 'labradorite' are explained by their context, and their technical precision suits the concentrated hardness of the poem.

'On the Ocean Floor' is almost equally successful in producing powerful reverberations in four lines:

> Now more and more on my concern with the lifted waves of
>   genius gaining
> I am aware of the lightless depths that beneath them lie;
> And as one who hears their tiny shells incessantly raining
> On the ocean floor as the foraminifera die.

The meaning of the crucial word 'foraminifera' might be guessed from the context, but the poem gains immensely if we know that these are minute primitive sea-creatures with beautiful chalky shells which are perforated in patterns, like old Chinese ivory balls; while the animal is alive its protoplasm extrudes in filaments through the fine holes in its shell, as it floats and swims through the water, and when it dies the protoplasm disappears and the empty shell falls slowly to the ocean floor. But the main point which drew MacDiarmid to make his analogy is that this creature is so numerous, millions upon millions drifting through the seas for millions of years, existing long before man came on the scene, that, small as it is, it has raised up through the passage of time huge chalk and limestone cliffs made from the shells. MacDiarmid is saying that he has been too self-centred, too concerned with the individual genius, the outstanding person, he had forgotten the great mass of ordinary mankind; but now, in the thirties, in the period of economic and political crisis, he suddenly becomes aware of what as a Communist he should be aware of—the masses themselves, dying and falling anonymously like the foraminifera, but from whom something is going to rise up, a new society, like the chalk cliffs rising from the depths of the sea. So this poem too could be called 'the skeleton of the future'. But for the slightly awkward inversions in the first two lines, this would be—and it nearly is—a masterly little poem.

Fond of testing things to extremes, MacDiarmid shoots a battery of geological terms into 'Stony Limits', his elegy on Charles Doughty (well, Doughty was a geologist as well as a poet and an explorer), or scatters a wide range of varied but extremely unfamiliar words in 'Vestigia Nulla Retrorsum', his elegy on Rilke (well, was Rilke not a difficult poet?), or strains every nerve to show the plenitude of the Scots vocabulary in 'Water Music' and 'Scots Unbound' (well, is it not the age of James Joyce?).

> (Wrang-heidit? Mm. *But heidit! That's the thing.*)
> (*To Circumjack Cencrastus*)

Certainly 'Stony Limits' does give a good impression of Doughty and his Arabia, even if one has some vagueness about xenolites and nicols, and 'Water Music' really is water music, an onomatopoeic display of the movements and sounds of brisk Border rivers. At the same time the reader is made aware that unless he has access to a very good dictionary his understanding of the poem is going to be incomplete, impressionistic; he has to decide if the comprehension is worth the effort. It is easiest to like a poem where a technical process is described in not too technical terms, though one is aware that in such cases MacDiarmid's new thrust towards science is modest. 'Crystals Like Blood' (published in 1949) is about the industrial process of the extraction of mercury from the red ore of cinnabar, about the iron piledrivers crumbling the ore while a conveyor draws it up into a huge grey-white kiln.

> So I remember how mercury is got
> When I contrast my living memory of you
> And your dear body rotting here in the clay
> —And feel once again released in me
> The bright torrents of felicity, naturalness, and faith
> My treadmill memory draws from you yet.

And whether the extraction of mercury is merely an extended metaphor in an elegy, or whether it is there as of interest in itself, seems about equally balanced. It is at least in part a 'poetry of knowledge'.

However, the volumes from the 1930s, and magazines from the same period, contain a considerable variety of poem: impressively ranging meditations like 'On a Raised Beach', 'Lament for the Great Music', 'Tarras', and 'Whuchulls'; strong personal poems like 'Of John Davidson', 'At my Father's Grave', and 'Kinsfolk'; satires like 'Prayer for a Second Flood'; hard little sociopolitical outbursts like 'Reflections in an Ironworks' and 'Another Epitaph on an Army of Mercenaries'; fine lyrics like 'Milk-wort and Bog-cotton'. 'On a Raised Beach' is perhaps the most impressive of these poems, and in its obstinate questioning of the unanswering—the million-year-old stones of a beach, which (like the eemis stane) could tell us so much about our prehistory if we had any means of unlocking their secrets— it brings out the most original, the most bleak, the most deeply speculative aspect of the author, and well repays study.

After the thirties, MacDiarmid's main volumes of poetry were *A Kist of Whistles* (1947), *In Memoriam James Joyce* (1955), *The Kind of Poetry I Want* (1961), and *Collected Poems* (1962, revised edition 1967). In addition, large extracts of poetry are included in *Lucky Poet* (1943), his autobiography. There is much overlapping, and much non-chronological grouping, in these books and in the other small volumes which followed the *Collected Poems*; poems will appear in differing versions, or will sometimes be separate and sometimes part of a larger work; both bibliographically and aesthetically, the later poetry bristles with problems.

As seen most extensively in *In Memoriam James Joyce* and *The Kind of Poetry I Want*, this poetry has had a mixed reception from readers and critics. The general verdict is probably, on the whole, still unfavourable, but there are signs of greater interest, and these are likely to grow stronger. What dismayed admirers of the earlier MacDiarmid was the turning from Scots to English, the deliberately prosaic tone, the widespread use of catalogues, often of recondite things, the apparently perverse refusal to transmute factual material into 'poetry'. Also, as more and more of this verse was found to be derived, with or without acknowledgement, and usually with little alteration except for the line-divisions, from passages of discursive prose in books and periodicals, the critic's pen has been inhibited, uncertain whether it would be praising (or dispraising) MacDiarmid or someone else. (An entertaining though inconclusive correspondence on MacDiarmid's alleged 'plagiarism' sprang up in *The Times Literary Supplement* between January and May 1965.) To mention two instances of 'derived' material: an impressive passage towards the end of *In Memoriam James Joyce* (p. 143), dealing with the development of the human embryo, is taken from Sir Charles Sherrington's *Man on his Nature* (1940), and almost the whole of the poem 'When the Birds come back to Rhiannon', which explores Celtic myth and the Celtic psyche, comes from Angus Robertson's *Children of the Fore-World* (1933). The poet playing the part of a Border reiver[1] into prose country, bringing back booty which he then sets up in his own way in his own house, is not in itself a new conception, as many examples from Shakespeare to Eliot and Robert Lowell would show; the difference lies in the extent, and one might say the passion, of MacDiarmid's depredations. Perhaps one should give him the 'traditional' defence Charles Olson gave to Herman Melville: 'He was a skald [Norse bard], and knew how to appropriate the work of others.'[2] He himself has defended his practice on two grounds: that work on such a large scale as most of his later poetry can stand the inclusion of foreign matter within its broad contextual scope, and that in any case he has always used a 'strong solution of books' because of his dislike of over-simple or sentimental poetry. These grounds will not please everybody, yet in view of the incorporative practices of other twentieth-century writers such as Ezra Pound, William Carlos Williams, David Jones, and William Burroughs, MacDiarmid's creative mosaics may not seem so eccentric as they are sometimes thought to be. David Jones, in his preface to *The Anathemata* (1952),

---

[1] Raider.
[2] *Call me Ishmael*, 1967, p. 37.

admiringly quotes from Nennius's *Historia Brittonum*: 'I have made a heap of all that I could find.' The love of multiplicity, and the recording of it, may link MacDiarmid to his age in a way that is very different from more obvious parallels such as that between his early lyrics and Imagism.

Language, evolution, and world-consciousness are the main concerns of the later poetry. In *In Memoriam James Joyce* MacDiarmid compares the innovative adventures of himself and Joyce in the world of words to the hard physical exploration of the Greenland ice-cap:

> We fumble along with partially bandaged eyes
> Our reindeer-skin kamiks worn into holes
> And no fresh sedge-grass to stump them with.
> We come on ice-fields like mammoth ploughlands
> And mountainous séracs which would puzzle an Alpine
>   climber.
> That is what adventuring in dictionaries means,
> All the abysses and altitudes of the mind of man,
> Every test and trial of the spirit,
> Among the débris of all past literature
> And raw material of all the literature to be.

kamiks: Eskimo boots   *séracs:* ice pinnacles

Human evolution, the poem argues, is hindered by the non-communicative diversity of cultures and languages, by the difficulty of making any concerted worldwide advance. Things that could wonderfully contribute to that advance remain isolated and unknown. The writer's job should be to help to bring languages and cultures closer together, to confront and confront until the new creative sparks appear. To anyone who is at all sympathetic to these ideas, the poem can prove stimulating, and even exhilarating. Stuffed to indigestibility as it sometimes is with fact and reference, it nevertheless reveals the true passion of the author for the materials he has chosen to use, and its attempt at a poetry of knowledge, however faulty its execution, is not negligible.

The Kind of Poetry I Want proceeds by a series of analogies to define the kind of poetry MacDiarmid would particularly want as a counter-force to what he sees as the 'soggily and indiscriminately affectionate' nature of most post-Burnsian Scottish poetry—'like a dog when it loves you'. He dreams of 'poems like the bread-knife / Which cuts three slices at once', of 'poetry that goes all the way / From Brahma to a stock', of poetry like bending a piece of wire 'backwards and forwards until it breaks', of 'a poetry which fully understands / That the era of technology is a necessary fact', and above all of

> a learned poetry, knowing how
> Taliesin[1] received the hazel rod
> From the dying hand of Virgil
> Who in his turn had taken it from Homer.

From his own evidence it would also be an open-ended poetry, little concerned to give the pleasures of tight construction, but wishing constantly to refresh the reader through surprise. Like the would-be circumjacker of Cencrastus the Curly Snake, or like Varuna riding the sea-monster in *In Memoriam James Joyce*, the reader of the kind of poetry MacDiarmid wants must be willing to take a plunge into elusive, kaleidoscopically shifting territory where the straight line is unknown.

Most observers of MacDiarmid's work are struck by its curious mixing of desire to bring poetry and science together, on the one hand, and on the other hand the recurring element of metaphysical speculation. The former seems to be aligned with his love of the multitudinousness of things, the latter with his equally deep interest in the desolate, the barren, the remote, and the solitary. Like his hero Charles Doughty, who combined minute geological and linguistic detail with far-ranging visions of Arabia, Britain, time, myth, and history, MacDiarmid comes to us swathed in the Many yet yearning towards the One. If many of his poems are cascades of particularities, others are in praise of an almost mystical emptiness, deprivation, withdrawal, silence, and stillness. One of the oddest of his poems, though attractive and important as well as odd, itself comments on this point. 'Esplumeoir' is about eternity, and is written in the form of a one-sided dialogue with an

[1] A Welsh bard who flourished in the sixth century AD.

unenlightened questioner who fears that that state would be dull and inhuman. But MacDiarmid feels the magnetic pull of the 'esplumeoir'—the magic cave where Merlin lay bewitched by Vivien—and looks forward to eternity's bewitching, non-sensuous, yet intensely perceived vacancy.

> Eternity's like that—a'thing keyed up
> To the heichest pitch as if
> A cataclysm's comin'—only it's no!

heichest: highest

Entering eternity, you do not find it outwardly impressive. It is a small white building with shutters and a canopy.

> The canopy's royal blue
> And it says *Eternity*
> In discreet soap-glass letters
> On ilka-side. Under the canopy
> You walk up and the front door
> Is a' mirror wi' a cool strip
> O' fluorescent light on top.
> You push the pearl button,
> And listen to the delicate chimes
> And adjust your tie in the mirror
> And fix your hat—but the guy
> Ahint the bullet-proof mirror
> Sees a' that too,
> Only you canna see him.

ilka: each   *Ahint:* behind

The doorman, who turns out to be a big white-haired black, admits you if he approves, you check your hat in a 'quiet soft-lit anteroom', and then the whole place is yours. Indescribable except in terms of coolness, quietness, stillness, and simplicity, eternity at first sight appears blank, but it is a blankness that conceals pure energy, intelligence, and undistracted meditation. 'Don't imagine the Grail contains pike, lamprey, or salmon,' as Perceval was warned in Arthurian legend.

Austere grail—and teeming cornucopia. MacDiarmid's poetry suggests both, and this is no doubt one of the reasons —though far from the only one—why he is so hard to

27

categorize or evaluate. Critical disagreements are likely to be rife for some time to come, whenever his exact place in Scottish and general twentieth-century poetry is discussed. But it should be impossible to deny the force, vividness, and illumination of his best poetry, quite as remarkable in its way as the work of contemporaries like Eliot and Pound, even while admitting that there is a great range between his best and his worst. His own awareness of what is basically the problem of the very prolific writer was nicely expressed in 1964 in a letter to George Bruce, the poet and (then) BBC producer: 'My job, as I see it, has never been to lay a tit's egg, but to erupt like a volcano emitting not only flame but a lot of rubbish.'[1] The sense of extremes shown by his choice of the images of tit's egg and volcanic eruption is highly characteristic of the man. His work mingles the prophetic and the opportunistic, vision and serendipity, to an unusual degree, and it would not be surprising if some of his effects came off and others did not. What he would never want is a static or formal theory of art. He has never believed that art can be relegated from the general evolutionary stream (full of hopeful mutations and choppy setbacks as that is) to a backwater, however warm and consolatory, of 'permanent' human feelings. Art, as he sees it, ought to be a metamorphosing force in its own right, with a duty to advance, and in advancing to advance man's spirit. That this should happen particularly through *language*, and that the poet should be its most convincing exponent, follows naturally from the fact that language is man's most distinctive evolutionary instrument. It is a restatement, after Darwin and Lamarck, of the Shelleyan position: that poets are 'the mirrors of the gigantic shadows which futurity casts upon the present'. Hugh MacDiarmid's mirror may have some Shandean kinks in the glass, and be in need of polishing here and there, but it remains a powerful and astonishing transmitter.

[1] Quoted in the catalogue of the MacDiarmid exhibition, National Library of Scotland, Edinburgh, 1967.

Much of MacDiarmid's life was spent as a working journalist, and it would be unlikely that the vigour of his
mind should not show itself in works of prose as well as of
verse. Because the bulk of his prose has been until recent-
ly inaccessible in out-of-print books or out-of-the-way
journals (and much of it still is), the remarkable variety of
his contributions in this area has been undervalued. The two
useful collections edited by Kenneth Buthlay (*The Uncanny
Scot*, 1968) and Duncan Glen (*Selected Essays*, 1969) bring
together a wide range of scattered essays, sketches, and
stories, and between them give a very fair sampling of
MacDiarmid's prose. It is worth remembering that his first
book, *Annals of the Five Senses* (1923), was a prose work
(though it also contained some poems): an acutely self-
conscious series of essays and sketches and reminiscences and
meditations, written in a packed, rich, contorted, un-
comfortable, deliberately experimental style, and already, in
its fondness for producing a mosaic of quotations, fore-
shadowing developments that were to surface many years
later. As he wrote in the preface:

As fish are seen through an aquarium so these perhaps strange
fish of mine are discernible almost entirely through a 'strong
solution of books'—and not only of books but of magazines and
newspaper articles and even of speeches. What I have done is
similar to what is done when a green light on a railway replaces
a red light, or *vice versa*, in a given lamp.

The importance of *Annals of the Five Senses* is that it showed
MacDiarmid establishing his *bona fides* as a modern, and
indeed modernist writer, quite apart from any interests he
may have had in specifically Scottish or specifically political
matters. But the chief impact he made on the public
through his prose came, as one would expect, from his more
direct and more controversial writing. He never ceased to
attack those persons and institutions (not without having
made use of them where necessary) that he regarded as
deadweight establishments ripe for a well-placed kick into
history, and in the same way he kept an eager eye for every

new development in Britain or abroad that held out promise of forward-moving values. The series of sprightly articles he wrote for *The Scottish Educational Journal* between 1925 and 1927 (partly collected as *Contemporary Scottish Studies* in 1926, reissued more fully under the same title, together with the correspondence they provoked, in 1976) offer the strongest proof we have of the confidence of the new broom, of the man who mounts the *Zeitgeist* at the right moment and points the fresh paths which are in fact the ones that are going to be taken. Whether savaging Mrs Kennedy-Fraser's sentimentally doctored *Songs of the Hebrides* of early this century in comparison with the enlightened and scientific use of folk-song by Bartók and Kodály in Hungary, or prophetically recommending young Scottish writers like Edwin Muir and Neil Gunn at the expense of established favourites such as Charles Murray and Neil Munro, or pleading for an end to the 'sabotage' of true cultural and intellectual values by an increasingly utilitarian education system, MacDiarmid impresses by his indefatigable concern to cause change, to undermine provincialism, sloth, and complacence, to expose the old guard and get them to condemn themselves through their own self-defence, as frequently happened in the correspondence columns. He was not right in everything, but a reader today is surprised to see how often he was, and how sharply at that time—the time also of his creative achievement in *Sangschaw* and *A Drunk Man Looks at the Thistle*—his critical faculties uncovered the significant roots of the matters he was discussing.

Other books continued the struggle, on a number of fronts. *Albyn, or Scotland and the Future* (1927) speculated on how Scottish national identity could best thrive, and had interesting things to say about the extension of the 'Scottish Renaissance' from literary into general cultural and political areas of operation: an extension with baffling setbacks. 'Scotland is unique among European nations in its failure to develop a nationalist sentiment strong enough to be a vital factor in its affairs.' To find ways of removing this unenviable diffidence should be the educated Scotsman's task. *At the Sign of the Thistle* (1934) was a collection of essays ranging in material from 'Gertrude Stein' to 'English

Ascendancy in British Literature' and 'The Case for Synthetic Scots'. MacDiarmid and Stein might seem an unlikely combination, but what attracted him to her work was its dryness, its impersonality, its being 'at the opposite extreme from all literature that depends upon inducing hyperaesthesia'. No doubt he enlists her for his own purposes, as he enlists Dostoevsky or Shestov or Rilke or Spengler or William Dunbar, but at the same time it is characteristic of his unconventional approach to criticism, and consonant with his anti-provincial polemic, to make sure that readers expecting nationalist debate ('At the sign of the Thistle', as the title says) will also be exposed to Stein—and to Valéry and Cocteau and Joyce too. Some name-dropping is involved; yet even gestures, given a cloggingly conservative cultural situation, can have point.

In the same year as *At the Sign of the Thistle* there appeared the mixed bag of prose and verse he produced in conjunction with the novelist Lewis Grassic Gibbon: *Scottish Scene, or the Intelligent Man's Guide to Albyn*. MacDiarmid's essays, sketches, poems, and playlets in this book, often ironic and humorous, are worth reading in themselves, but gain in their juxtaposition to Gibbon's contributions and to the running 'newsreel' of contemporary news-items; the volume is one that is valuable for its tart flavour of the Scottish thirties.

Although some of the prose books are of slight importance—*The Islands of Scotland* (1939) being notable mainly for its first publication of the unintentionally plagiarized poem 'Perfect' which gave rise to the lengthy *Times Literary Supplement* correspondence of 1965 and which is now excised from the *Collected Poems* (replaced, with an impishness, or forgetfulness, that can only be called sublime, by a 'poem' lifted from Hart Crane's *The Bridge*), and *Burns Today and Tomorrow* (1959) being not much more than a handy gathering together and restatement of his views already expressed on Burns and the Burns cult—others yield more interest than they seem to hold out. *Scottish Eccentrics* (1936) is a collection of essays, on expected figures like Sir Thomas Urquhart, William McGonagall, and Lord Monboddo and on others less expected, the essays relying heavily on quotations from earlier biographers and commentators; but here the whole is greater than the parts, with the gradual building up of an argument about desirable and undesirable traits of national character, and an emerging polemic against the widespread idea of the 'canny Scot' and in favour of the 'uncanny Scot'. Not only does he see and recommend 'the persistence of the wayward, antinomian Scottish type—versatile, erudite, filled with wanderlust spiritual and physical, indifferent to or incapable of mere worldly prudence', but he goes further, to Shestov, to find 'that frontier beyond which the might of general ideas ceases' as the true frontier for the eccentric, impulsive Scottish genius. Against the hardheaded business or political world of the 'Scotsman on the make' he sets elusive spiritual values drawn almost out of the air. The failed Urquhart has likelier access than the successful John Buchan to the secret movements of Cencrastus.

If we have not yet 'caught' MacDiarmid, surely we shall catch him in his autobiography? *Lucky Poet* (1943; reissued 1972 with a new 'author's note') had the warning subtitle 'A Self-Study in Literature and Political Ideas, being the Autobiography of Hugh MacDiarmid', and here we are not to look for any straight chronological unfolding of the events of his life or for any deep, troubled, psychological self-examination. It is a unique book, chaotic, repetitive, careless in every kind of detail, yet bursting with suggestive ideas, curious facts, instant flytings, brilliant analogies, and pages of *vers libre* looming like extracts from that huge Shelleyan poem 'which all poets, like the co-operating thoughts of one great mind, have built up since the beginning of the world.'[1] Much of the poetry appears in *The Kind of Poetry I Want* and elsewhere; the ideas on literature, politics, and science, the Anglophobia and the world-consciousness, the mosaic method of composition using 'hundreds of thousands of newspaper cuttings', all these are familiar; yet the total impossible montage of this non-autobiography betrays in each twist and turn so many of the traits of its compiler, that in the end we can see why he himself regards it as his 'next most important book' after the

[1] Shelley, *A Defence of Poetry*.

32

Drunk Man. A sequel to it, published in 1966 as *The Company I've Kept*, is less interesting.

In prose as in verse, it is a kind of irrepressible energy that strikes us most in MacDiarmid's work, an energy which at times outruns the reader's patience or the demands of the subject but which always recovers unexpectedly, pauses, and strikes like a cobra. His methods are his own, and he is a model for no one, but he is one of the great twentieth-century writers, and a writer whose individuality it will take the next century to sift and define.

HUGH MACDIARMID

A Select Bibliography

(Place of publication London, unless stated otherwise)

Bibliographies

'Hugh MacDiarmid: a first checklist', by W. R. Aitken, *The Biblio-theck* (Glasgow), 1, 4, Autumn 1958.

HUGH MACDIARMID AND THE SCOTTISH RENAISSANCE, by Duncan Glen; Edinburgh (1964)

—contains 'Hugh MacDiarmid: A Chronological Bibliography'.

THE LITERARY MASKS OF HUGH MACDIARMID, by Duncan Glen; Glasgow (1964)

—limited edition.

'Hugh MacDiarmid: a second checklist', by W. R. Aitken. *The Bibliotheck* (Aberdeen), 5, 7-8, 1970.

A SMALL PRESS AND HUGH MACDIARMID, with a checklist of *Akros* publications, 1962-70, by Duncan Glen; Preston (1970).

HUGH MACDIARMID: A Critical Survey, ed. Duncan Glen; Edinburgh (1972)

—includes 'A Hugh MacDiarmid Bibliography', by W. R. Aitken.

Collected Editions:

STONY LIMITS AND SCOTS UNBOUND, AND OTHER POEMS; Edinburgh (1956).

THREE HYMNS TO LENIN; Edinburgh (1957). *Verse*

COLLECTED POEMS; New York (1962).

—revised ed., 1967.

A LAP OF HONOUR (1967). *Verse*

A CLYACK-SHEAF (1969). *Verse*

MORE COLLECTED POEMS (1970).

Selections:

SELECTED POEMS (1934).

SELECTED POEMS OF HUGH MACDIARMID, ed. R. Crombie Saunders; Glasgow (1944).

SPEAKING FOR SCOTLAND: Selected Poems; Baltimore (1946).

SELECTED POEMS OF HUGH MACDIARMID, ed. Oliver Brown; Glasgow (1954).

THE UNCANNY SCOT: A Selection of Prose, ed. Kenneth Buthlay (1968).

SELECTED ESSAYS OF HUGH MACDIARMID, edited with an introduction by
  Duncan Glen (1969).
SELECTED POEMS, selected and edited by David Craig and John Manson;
  Harmondsworth (1970).
THE HUGH MACDIARMID ANTHOLOGY: Poems in Scots and English, ed.
  Michael Grieve and Alexander Scott (1972).

Separate Works:

  ANNALS OF THE FIVE SENSES; Montrose (1923). *Prose and verse*
  SANGSCHAW; Edinburgh (1925). *Verse*
  PENNY WHEEP; Edinburgh (1926). *Verse*
  A DRUNK MAN LOOKS AT THE THISTLE; Edinburgh (1926). *Verse*
  —later edns: Glasgow, 1953; Edinburgh 1956, 1962; Amherst, Mass.,
    ed. John C. Weston, 1971.
  CONTEMPORARY SCOTTISH STUDIES (1926). *Prose*
  —reissued with additional material, Edinburgh, 1976.
  ALBYN, OR SCOTLAND AND THE FUTURE (1927). *Prose*
  TO CIRCUMJACK CENCRASTUS, or, The Curly snake; Edinburgh (1930).
    Verse
  FIRST HYMN TO LENIN, AND OTHER POEMS (1931).
  SECOND HYMN TO LENIN; Thakeham [1932]. *Verse*
  SCOTS UNBOUND, AND OTHER POEMS; Stirling (1932).
  STONY LIMITS, AND OTHER POEMS (1934).
  AT THE SIGN OF THE THISTLE: A Collection of essays [1934]. *Prose*
  FIVE BITS OF MILLER (1934). *Prose*
  SCOTTISH SCENE (1934). *Prose and verse*
  —with Lewis Grassic Gibbon; reissued, Bath 1974.
  SECOND HYMN TO LENIN AND OTHER POEMS (1935)
  —contains new poems.
  SCOTTISH ECCENTRICS (1936). *Prose*
  —reissued, New York, 1972.
  THE ISLANDS OF SCOTLAND: Hebrides, Orkneys, and Shetlands (1939).
    Prose
  LUCKY POET (1943). *Prose*
  —reissued, 1972.
  CORNISH HEROIC SONG FOR VALDA TREVLYN; Glasgow [1943].
  A KIST OF WHISTLES: New poems; Glasgow [1947].
  CUNNINGHAME GRAHAM: A Centenary Study; Glasgow [1952]. *Prose*
  FRANCIS GEORGE SCOTT: An Essay; Edinburgh (1955). *Prose*
  IN MEMORIAM JAMES JOYCE: From a vision of world language; Glasgow
    (1955). *Verse*
  THE BATTLE CONTINUES; Edinburgh (1957). *Verse*
  —an attack on Roy Campbell.

BURNS TODAY AND TOMORROW; Edinburgh (1959). *Prose*

THE KIND OF POETRY I WANT; Edinburgh (1961). *Verse*

DAVID HUME: Scotland's greatest son; Edinburgh [1962]. *Prose*
—a lecture given at Edinburgh University, April 1961.

THE MAN OF (ALMOST) INDEPENDENT MIND; Edinburgh (1962). *Prose*
—a study of David Hume.

THE UGLY BIRDS WITHOUT WINGS; Edinburgh (1962). *Prose*

SYDNEY GOODSIR SMITH; Edinburgh (1963). *Prose*

POEMS TO PAINTINGS BY WILLIAM JOHNSTONE, 1933; Edinburgh (1963).

THE TERRIBLE CRYSTAL: A Vision of Scotland; Skelmorlie (1964)
—two poems.

THE MINISTRY OF WATER: Two poems; Glasgow (1964).

THE FIRE OF THE SPIRIT: Two poems; Glasgow (1965).

THE COMPANY I'VE KEPT (1966). *Prose*

WHUCHULLS: A Poem; Preston (1966).

EARLY LYRICS BY HUGH MACDIARMID, ed. J. K. Annand; Preston (1968)
Verse and prose

A POLITICAL SPEECH; Edinburgh (1972). *Prose*

SONG OF THE SERAPHIM (1973)
—limited edition.

DIREADH I, II, AND III; Pitlochry (1974)
—limited edition.

JOHN KNOX; Edinburgh (1976)
—with Campbell Maclean and Anthony Ross.

Works edited, translated, adapted, etc.

NORTHERN NUMBERS: Being representative selections from certain living Scottish poets, edited by Hugh MacDiarmid; Edinburgh (1920)
—second series, Edinburgh 1921; third series, Montrose 1922.

THE GOLDEN TREASURY OF SCOTTISH POETRY, selected and edited by Hugh MacDiarmid (1940)
—with extensive and idiosyncratic introduction and notes.

ANIARA: A Review of man in time and space, by Harry Martinson (1963)
—adapted from the Swedish by Hugh MacDiarmid and Elspeth Harley Schubert.

THE THREEPENNY OPERA, by Bertolt Brecht (1973)
—translated from the German by Hugh MacDiarmid.

Records:

HUGH MACDIARMID READS HIS OWN POETRY; Claddagh Records: Dublin (1969).
—includes a very clear prose statement of his aims by the poet.

A DRUNK MAN LOOKS AT THE THISTLE: HUGH MACDIARMID READS HIS
OWN POEM; Claddagh Records: Dublin (1970).
Both records have sleeve notes by Alexander Scott.

Interviews:

With Magnus Magnusson, *The Scotsman*, (Edinburgh), 12 August,
1967.

With Duncan Glen, *Akros* (Preston), 5, 13, April 1970.

With George Bruce, *Akros* (Preston), 5, 13, April 1970.

With Walter Perrie, published as pamphlet, *Hugh MacDiarmid:
Metaphysics and Poetry*; Hamilton (1975).

Scottish Marxist (Glasgow), 10, Winter 1975.

Some Critical Studies:

'Le groupe de "la Renaissance Écossaise"', by Denis Saurat, *La
Revue Anglo-Américaine:* Première Année, 4, April 1924.

'The Poetry of Hugh MacDiarmid', by William Soutar, *The Free
Man*, 3, 10, 7 April 1934.

'Hugh MacDiarmid: Scotland's Vortex-maker', by A. C. Frost, *The
Bookman*, 86, 516, September 1934.

'Hugh MacDiarmid—Second Hymn to Lenin', by F. R. Leavis,
Scrutiny: 4, 3, December 1935.

SCOTT AND SCOTLAND: The Predicament of the Scottish writer, by
Edwin Muir (1936).

'The Thistle in the Lion's Mouth', by R. Crombie Saunders, *Life and
Letters Today*, 44, 91, March 1945.

'PLASTIC SCOTS' AND THE SCOTTISH LITERARY TRADITION, by Douglas
Young, [Glasgow 1947].

'Hugh MacDiarmid and Scottish Poetry', by David Daiches, *Poetry*
(Chicago), 72, 4, July 1948.

THE SCOTTISH RENAISSANCE, by Maurice Lindsay; Edinburgh (1948).

'The Poetry of Hugh MacDiarmid', by Mary Baird Aitken, *Scottish
Art and Letters*, 4, [1949].

'Introduction' to *A Drunk Man looks at the Thistle*, by David Daiches;
Glasgow (1953)

—also printed in Edinburgh edns. of 1956 and 1962.

'The Scottish Renaissance', by Geoffrey Wagner, *The Adelphi*, 30, 1,
Fourth Quarter, 1953.

'MacDiarmid's New Poem', by David Daiches, *Lines Review*, 9,
August 1955.

'Hugh MacDiarmid's Poetry', by David Craig, *The Voice of Scotland*,
7, 1, April 1956.

'Jujitsu for the Educated', by Edwin Morgan, *The Twentieth Century*, 160, 955, September 1956.

'Scarlet Eminence', by Burns Singer, *Encounter*, 8, 3, March 1957.

THE SCOTTISH TRADITION IN LITERATURE, by Kurt Wittig; Edinburgh (1958).

HUGH MACDIARMID: A festschrift, ed. K. D. Duval and Sydney Goodsir Smith; Edinburgh (1962)

—contains essays by Walter Keir, David Daiches, George Bruce, Sydney Goodsir Smith, David Craig, Douglas Young, Douglas Sealy, Edwin Morgan, Ronald Stevenson, A. T. Cunninghame, Albert Mackie, Helen B. Cruickshank, and Maurice Lindsay, and a checklist by William R. Aitken.

'MacDiarmid and Sherrington', by Edwin Morgan, *Notes and Queries*, n.s. 10, 10, October 1963.

THE GOLDEN LYRIC: An essay on the poetry of Hugh MacDiarmid, by Iain Crichton Smith; Preston (1967)

—limited edition.

Agenda. Double issue on Hugh MacDiarmid and Scottish Poetry. 5, 4-6, 1, Autumn-Winter 1967-68.

—contains essays by Tom Scott, John Montague, William Cookson, Alexander Scott, Duncan Glen, Hugo Moore, Kenneth Cox, and Matthew P. McDiarmid.

'Hugh MacDiarmid and the "Poetry of Fact"', by R. B. Watson, *Stand*, 9, 4, 1968.

Akros. Double issue on Hugh MacDiarmid. 5, 13-14, April 1970.

—contains interviews by Duncan Glen and George Bruce, essays by Duncan Glen, J. K. Annand, T. S. Law, Arno Reinfrank, G. S. Fraser, John Herdman, and Roderick Watson, and bibliographical notes by Duncan Glen.

'The Side-Road to Dunsyre: Some comments on Hugh MacDiarmid and Ian Hamilton Finlay', by Stephen Scobie, *Akros*, 5, 15, August 1970.

HUGH MACDIARMID'S 'A DRUNK MAN LOOKS AT THE THISTLE'. An essay, by John C. Weston, Preston (1970).

HUGH MACDIARMID: A Critical Survey, ed. Duncan Glen; Edinburgh (1972)

—contains essays by Alexander Scott, Duncan Glen, Burns Singer, David Daiches, John C. Weston, Roderick Watson, Matthew P. McDiarmid, Iain Crichton Smith, Sydney Goodsir Smith, David Craig, Douglas Sealy, Tom Scott, Edwin Morgan, Michel Habart, and G. S. Fraser, and a bibliography by W. R. Aitken.

THE MACDIARMID MAKARS, 1923-1972, by Alexander Scott; Preston (1972).

'The Appreciation of the Golden Lyric: Early Scots Poems of Hugh MacDiarmid', by Kenneth Buthlay, *Scottish Literary Journal*, 2, 1, July 1975.

'A look at the Langholm Thistle', by Ruth McQuillan, *Calgacus*, 1, 3, Spring 1976.

POEMS OF HUGH MACDIARMID. Read by Kenneth Buthlay, Sandy Ross, Eleanor Aitken, and Edwin Morgan; Scotsoun Cassettes: Glasgow (1976). *2 cassettes*

—with an illuminating introduction and linking commentary by Kenneth Buthlay.

WRITERS AND THEIR WORK